New York Diary

Sibling Rivalry Press, LLC
PO Box 26147
Little Rock, AR 72221

info@siblingrivalrypress.com

www.siblingrivalrypress.com

ISBN: 978-1-943977-83-3

Library of Congress Control Number: 2020948982

By special invitation, this title is housed in the Rare Book and Special Collections Vault of the Library of Congress.

First Sibling Rivalry Press Edition, January 2021

New York Diary

Tim Dlugos

EDITED BY DAVID TRINIDAD

SIBLING RIVALRY PRESS

DISTURB/ENRAPTURE

LITTLE ROCK, ARKANSAS

EDITOR'S NOTE

WHEN TIM DLUGOS MOVED TO NEW YORK in June of 1976, he had already received acclaim as a poet in Washington, D.C., where he was a regular participant in the Mass Transit poetry scene. New York was the big leap, a way of raising the stakes and proving himself as a writer, and he would soon make a name for himself there as well. This diary, written in his first six months in the City That Never Sleeps, is a record of his immersion in the downtown poetry scene and a gay lifestyle that was then relentlessly promiscuous. From the very beginning, when he "gobbles up" some chocolate mints left behind by Joe Brainard, Tim is like Alice eating a cake that changes her size; he's off and running in a Wonderland of art openings and late-night escapades at the baths. During the subsequent months, he meets a great many people; he has a good deal of sex; he absorbs a great deal of culture. In early August, as he notes his twenty-sixth birthday, one realizes he is just a kid—a precocious one, but a youngster nonetheless.

Almost immediately, Tim complains that the pace of the city works against keeping a thorough diary. He's "writing things down here less and less"; he finds it "harder & harder to write here regularly." There are too many people, too many parties and poetry readings, too much alcohol, too much sex. The diary becomes unsustainable. As much as one wishes he'd been able to continue it, his poetry will require his full attention. His New York years will be prolific ones. Where the diary falls off, Tim's life as an artistic, sexual, and spiritual adventurer is channeled into his poems.

As with the drafts of his poetry, Tim wrote the diary on yellow legal pads. I first read it after he died of AIDS in 1990, but nearly thirty years would pass before I transcribed it (his poems took precedence in the interim). I have identified as many people as possible. Even with the help of Google and Tim's friends, some of them have fallen through the net. Others are now the stuff of legends. In the forty-four years that have elapsed since Tim wrote this diary, the world has changed several times over: AIDS, 9/11, Coronavirus. The New York that Tim captures in these pages is long gone. While it gives us a few precious glimpses of that lost world, his diary is a reminder of how quickly a world can disappear.

David Trinidad
Chicago, 2020

NEW YORK DIARY

3 June 1976 –

Sitting in new apartment, 4th-floor Kenward Elmslie's[1] house, on Greenwich Avenue in New York. Esther Phillips on stereo, sky outside clouding up. Joe Brainard[2] left some chocolate mint candy, which I've been gobbling up (washed down with Miller's High Life this early afternoon, Randy's[3] at the grocery buying lunch).

My intention in starting this is to keep it going—the last time I began a diary was when I went into Brothers,[4] so this must really be a bigger move than I think. I'd been meaning to start sooner, but paper and pens were packed up. Some things from last days in Washington to set down for posterity—

– call up Joe B to be sure he'll meet us in NY w/ keys to the house, and he answers the phone in foghorn voice, like Brando in *The Godfather*. Turns out he'd missed an appointment w/ the dentist & if it had been the office on the other end when he'd picked up the phone, he'd have said Mr. Brainard was not home.

– Going-away party at Terry Winch's,[5] with the people I love (and some who I didn't particularly care about one way or the other). Bill MacPherson[6] was there, which surprised me—he's one person I wish I'd gotten to know better.

---

1 Kenward Elmslie (1929-) Poet, performer, editor/publisher of *Z Magazine* and Z Press (1973-1977). Elmslie lived at 104 Greenwich Avenue.

2 Joe Brainard (1942-1994) Artist and writer.

3 Randy Russell. TD's boyfriend from Washington, D.C.

4 From 1968 to 1971, TD was a member of the Christian Brothers, a Roman Catholic religious order, when he lived in Arlington, VA, and later in Philadelphia, PA.

5 Terence Winch (1945-) Poet, writer, musician.

6 William MacPherson (1933-2017) Writer and journalist.

Kerry[7] took me out in corridor for many kisses—he told me he loves me, which brought lump to my throat, and that I'm one of the few people he trusts, which gave me huge West Point rush—"will never disappoint him," etc. Gorgeous Herschel Browne[8] was there too and Bernie,[9] whom I love. Huge surprise of evening was that Terry invited Ed Cox,[10] with whom he hasn't spoken in 2 years. They were cordial to each other. I was overwhelmed that my departure was the catalyst for their reunion, even if it was an incomplete one.

– Ralph[11] (*THE* Ralph) called me at work my last day there, told me that I'd done a good job, thanked me for my work with *Public Citizen* (I thanked him for "the opportunity") and said to "call us up" if I'm ever back in DC. And I will.

– Drove big truck (8900 lbs) down to NY. Moving a hassle—not much fun. But I told everyone for 3 days, "The men who drive the big rigs know."

– Bill Wallace[12] helped us move in (took him to Duff's afterward for dinner in thanks) & gave us needlepoint design

---

7   Kerry MacBride. An attractive blond young man who attended the Mass Transit poetry readings in Washington, D.C.

8   Herschel McKinley Browne III (1952-2018) Roommate and childhood friend of Bernard Welt. According to Terence Winch, "Herschel Browne was an intriguing character—sly, ironic, smart, mischievous . . . a very good poet. I remember getting a sheaf of sonnets by him either from him or Bernard & being impressed . . . I don't think he took himself seriously as a poet. Oh, and he was also a junkie. Not sure how deep into that he was, but I seem to remember that the drugs were pretty central for him."

9   Bernard Welt (1952-) Poet and writer.

10 Ed Cox (1946-1992) Poet.

11 Ralph Nader (1934-) Political activist, writer, attorney. From 1974 to 1976, TD worked as a fundraising assistant and editor of Nader's *Public Citizen* newspaper.

12 Friend of TD from the Christian Brothers.

he'd executed—went out w/ Rob[13] after dinner and ended up in rain at The Stud and The Strap, both of which were empty. Messed around w/ Rob a little—I look forward to sleeping w/ him again. [No sexual dysfunction up here at all—was totally un-horny the last wk. in DC & worried about it, (along with everything else in my future), but NYC has recharged the libido.]

– Steve Hamilton[14] called yesterday a.m., said he'd awakened in a strange apt. on Perry St. w/ an Indian man handing him a glass of pineapple juice—and he didn't remember how he got there. Gave Steve my bed to keep for the duration of our stay at Kenward's, then drove truck to 2nd St & 2nd Ave to drop it off, only to be told their lot was full and please drop it off at 11th Av & 42nd Street. *Such* a hassle to do *anything* in this city— I'm going to stay in the Village as much as possible.

Right now have to go to bank & cash money order—may go away this wknd., & may miss Irma Towle's[15] daughter's birthday party downstairs on Sunday. She was here to look the place over this morning—pleasant woman, afraid she'll inconvenience Trevor[16] or us. And Trevor, who reminds me of Ian Young[17] [who called last night to wish us well, a kind thing to do], jokingly let on that it *would* be an inconvenience. Too fucking bad.

Just looked inside this legal pad & noticed the 1st draft of my poem "Last Poem, First Morning" which I wrote on train on way home from NY after sleeping w/ Rob for first time—April 17, 1971. The same pad! If this is the beginning of something as happy and auspicious, I look forward to passing through.

---

13 Longtime boyfriend of TD.

14 Steve Hamilton. Poet.

15 Wife of poet Tony Towle.

16 Trevor Winkfield (1944-) Artist and writer.

17 Ian Young (1945-) Poet, editor, literary critic, historian.

Jun 4 –

Dinner w/ Jeff last night (spaghetti, here) then off for evening of consumer-oriented sex—first to bookstore on Chris St,[1] where the men in tiny booths were getting same kinds of critical glances as the porno mags in front, then to the International/Stud & back room, where Randy & I both indulged. Met man named Randy Something who lives down the street, born in British Honduras (teaches at CUNY), about my age, w/ funny deep English accent which I did not discover until after flesh interlock in dark room where very unsexy porn films were being shown. Sex reduces to a series of muscular spasms & a moment of intensity across the eyes here, effectively placing it in same secondary position in "life" as celibacy or any other askesis. Thinking this a.m. of Mother Cabrini, the Saint of Soho where we went to feast last night (St Anthony Fiesta) and got a heavy Sense of Neighborhood. Thinking also of arranging party this weekend, may or may not depending on nerve and energy. Also, sad that Rob will be away for most of the summer, in Bermuda and back on a weekly cruise ship . . . I was looking forward to spending more time w/ him (he woke us up at 11 this morning w/ the news). We're dining tonight at Mary's. Tentative cool feelings over Trevor downstairs; he doesn't seem overly friendly, but neither do we, I guess. Am going to bank now.

---

1   Christopher Street.

5 June –

Twilight, almost; quiet time. Randy sleeps in anticipation of night out. We're going to Michael[1] & Ana's[2] at 10, and Jane DeLynn[3] will be there too. Just reread her story "Glimpses" in an old issue of *Paris Review*; truly fine. Look forward to meeting her in person, may invite her to party tomorrow. Some key people won't be coming; Frank Tobin, for example, has to work. But John & David[4] will be there; also Michael & Ana, and (hopefully) Billy Brosnahan. Saw John at party for Bill Zavatsky[5] at Gotham last night; he looks well, the redness out of his face since he stopped drinking, but no more charming giddiness either. Ray DiPalma[6] saw him as he entered the gallery, said "Oh here comes the prize-winner" or something like that. There are elements of "holding court" now when King John, as Barbara Guest[7] calls him, enters the room. I'd be uncomfortable and flattered simultaneously if I were in his shoes—but mostly I'd just love it.

Went w/ Rob last night to his choice of restaurant, Hisae's Seasonal Kitchen, which serves ridiculously large portions of *everything* at low prices. Later went to Stud alone, where I ran into Richard Rindskopf[8] from DC and Frank Tobin. Got

---

1   Michael Lally (1942-) Poet and actor.

2   Ana Ross-Gongora. Companion of Michael Lally at the time. Writes Lally: "We moved from DC to live together in NYC in early 1975, my son and daughter came for the summer and my son never went back to DC and his mother and the lesbian feminist commune she was living in there . . . Ana worked as executive assistants or whatever they called it back then, i.e. in an office for some bigwig lawyer or mover and shaker, she was very glamorous and tough and independent and a pretty easy person to live with . . . and Kenward and John et al. adored her."

3   Jane DeLynn (1946-) Novelist.

4   Poet John Ashbery (1927-2017) and his partner David Kermani.

5   Bill Zavatsky (1943-) Poet, translator, jazz pianist.

6   Ray DiPalma (1943-2016) Poet.

7   Barbara Guest (1920-2006) Poet.

8   Richard L. Rindskopf (1952-2016).

rain check for sex from Richard, who told me I should have grabbed him a year and a half ago—but I remember him at that time as uninterested. Put it down to my basic shyness. This afternoon took subway uptown to see Rob's ship leave—and as we arrived after they allowed guests to board, that's exactly what happened. Afterwards, walked thru *West-Side-Story*-land to Gotham Book Mart & tried to find new book by Alfred Corn[9] (Sandy McClatchy's[10] lover) with no success. Now stereo of person in apt. next door is pounding through 2 brick walls into our living room. May write occupant a little note if it gets to be a habit.

Dream I've been thinking of for a couple of days (I had it Tuesday night)—I'm sitting next to swimming pool w/ Randy on 5th floor of our old building on Rhode Island Avenue in DC, where of course there was no pool. Two gorgeous blond kids walk in, and I start talking to them, sipping Randy's Coke as I do. They hail, one blond tells me, from Alternate Passes, N.M.—then I turn to look at Randy and he's crying.

---

9 Alfred Corn (1943-) Poet and essayist.

10 J.D. McClatchy (1945-2018) Poet and literary critic.

7 June –

Jane DeLynn is *terrific*, and I find her quite attractive, which of course means she's probably a lesbian—and she is. Met her w/ Arlene Ladden,[1] Adrianne Blue[2] & a painter named Helène[3] at Michael & Ana's Saturday. Adrianne is doing a book for McKay on "successful women," so I gave her Charlene's name. Next day Jane & Adrianne came to party at our house. John and David were there (John was in a quiet & gentle humor, although Ana thinks he's bored by not drinking); also Irma Towle whose daughter had a birthday party downstairs earlier in the day, Bill Wallace, Steve Hamilton w/ whom I probably would have ended up in bed (again) if Randy weren't here, Ray & Betsi,[4] Bruce Andrews,[5] Charlie Croce[6] (who says there's no job for me at the Philharmonic), Michael Andre[7] (sans Erika[8]), Jeff Sosnick[9] & his friend Gary Olde (w/ whom I want to go to bed) and Simon,[10] the messiest looking 21-year-old in history perhaps, despite his good heart. Miles Lally[11] came too & fell asleep. It was a long, and good, party—I got drunk & fell asleep after we'd gone to get hamburgs at The Buffalo Roadhouse. Had invited Steve back for

---

1 Arlene Ladden. Poet and professor. Classmate of Jane DeLynn at the University of Iowa.

2 Adrianne Blue (1942-) Writer who was dating Jane DeLynn at the time.

3 Helène Aylon (1931-) Artist.

4 Elizabeth Brandfass. Artist and designer. Wife of Ray DiPalma.

5 Bruce Andrews (1948-) Poet.

6 Charles Croce. Director of Public Relations at the New York Philharmonic from 1975 to 1978.

7 Michael Andre (1946-) Poet, critic, editor.

8 Erika Rothenberg (1950-) Artist. With husband Michael Andre, she edited *The Poets' Encyclopedia* (Unmuzzled Ox, 1979).

9 Jeffrey Sosnick (1951-) Broadway producer and former Director of Annual Giving at GLAAD (Gay & Lesbian Alliance Against Defamation).

10 Simon Schuchat (1954-) Poet.

11 Miles Lally (1969-) Son of Michael Lally.

coffee & I just conked out on him. This a.m. woke up hung over, took Maalox, wrote 4 pages of short story "Waffles" and trotted off uncertainly to lunch w/ Robert Herrick of National Gay Task Force,[12] to talk about a job in direct mail. Something may turn up there, but I'm not sure—they've got funding problems. Fell asleep in afternoon, woke up, called parents, visited Balducci's to buy dinner, prepared dinner for Randy & me. Then meditated & chanted Aum for awhile (good feeling; Randy was napping or I would have been self-conscious) & went for long walk in Village twilight. Ended up on Morton Street Pier watching sky & water trade off colors, tugboats go home, and a V of geese flying high above the river, making their noise. Two spaces in the formation were empty, so the V was really a √. Decided at 10 to go to Billy Brosnahan's party, which had started at 9; got there by subway (it's a nondescript building on West 34th) and sat quietly drinking Coke all evening, listening to the theater people be theater people. Was one interesting person there (outside of Billy)—Riva Persikoff, a dancer w/ the Pennsylvania Ballet who's been on leave doing freelance work w/ Eliot Feld.[13] I *liked* her, despite her self-consciousness. She kept mentioning famous first names, which isn't bad, but then she repeated each one 10 times—Kris this, Kris that (Kristofferson), Clive this, Clive that (Barnes), etc. When Barry (Manilow) came up, I thought I'd tell my story about what a pig he is in bed, but held my peace. We left at the same time and I walked her to 9th Avenue and helped her hail a cab—I think she was afraid I was going to get in too. No such luck, honey. One interesting note from the party is that Billy (who'll be in Kalamazoo for the summer doing summer stock) is obviously as interested in Joe O'Hare[14] as he is uninterested in me, on *that* level. I find it hard at this point (after 2½ years) to muster any emotion at all

---

12 Now the National LGBTQ Task Force.

13 Eliot Feld (1942-) Modern ballet choreographer, performer, teacher, director.

14 Friend of TD from La Salle College in Philadelphia. O'Hare appears at the end of TD's poem "G-9."

over that.

Tomorrow is the start of second week in NYC—and the big questions (Will I get a job? Will I "make" "it"? Whe-e-e-ere. Is love?) remain. Party for JA[15] at Fischbach[16] tomorrow night, though, which I'm looking forward to.

---

15 John Ashbery.

16 The Fischbach Gallery was founded by Marilyn Cole Fischbach in 1960 at 799 Madison Avenue in New York City. By June 1976, the art gallery had moved to 29 West 57th Street.

10 June 76

Much hot poop to transcribe tonight. First—the Fischbach party for John on Tuesday night was *such* fun. I wore white bell-bottom cuffed pants, black patent loafers, dark blue shirt w/ open collar & seersucker jacket—the reason I devote such attention to the matter is that I agonized for an hour over whether that was "dressy" enough. We arrived at same time as Michael & Ana and John and David, so it was one grand entrance. Met some people I knew (Sandy McClatchy, Jimmy Schuyler,[1] Steven B. Hamilton), some people I didn't know (Lita Hornick,[2] fascinatingly ugly, Sandy's lover Alfred Corn, a very handsome gentle-seeming man, David Rosenberg,[3] who confirmed what everybody says about him, and fell totally in love with one Brad Gooch.[4] He's a little younger than I, with dark curly hair, stunningly attractive, and was seemingly "with" J.J. Mitchell,[5] a former lover of O'Hara[6] who was standing next to him on Fire Island the night he was run over (what a terrible way to be introduced, even behind your back!) JJ is apparently into S&M, so that's a very interesting little scene. Checked phone book when I got home, found Brad has 2 numbers listed. Danced a little with Ana, a lot with Michael, one last dance with Brad honey (I doubt it was reciprocal, sob) then trundled home. John was in

---

1 James Schuyler (1923-1991) Poet and writer.

2 Lita Hornick (1927-2000) Editor, publisher, art collector. Edited *Kulchur* magazine (1961-65) and Kulchur Press.

3 David Rosenberg (1943-) Poet, biblical translator, editor, educator.

4 Brad Gooch (1952-) Poet and writer.

5 J.J. Mitchell. Per Brad Gooch: "J.J. was a kind of golden boy; he went to Harvard, wrote poems, made pastels and was a brilliant talker. He also pissed his life away without ever applying himself to any career or leaving behind any cultural artifacts when he died of AIDS." Mitchell appears in TD's poems "G-9" and "The Bar." See also Thom Gunn's poem "Famous Friends" in *Boss Cupid*.

6 Frank O'Hara (1926-1966) Poet, writer, art critic.

fine form, holding court; and Aladar Marberger,[7] the co-host, was hilariously flitting (the word is sexist, but totally accurate) around making sure everyone had a good time. Michael Teague from DC, who I suspect is in British Intelligence, was there too.

Next a.m., luncheon here w/ Barbara Baracks.[8] She brought good wine; I bought good sandwiches; we talked about her manuscript I'm publishing. She's still in her late adolescent trauma, and I *like* her, despite her pushiness, which is however never malevolent. She's a Good Soul, I think, in the serious sense. Her work's uneven, but it's *her*, and I like that; there's the same excuse for publishing it as there was for SOUP putting out *High There*.[9]

Tonight I made my first literary enemy in DC—Bruce Andrews was reading to a very hard audience at a bar called Sobossek's, and the damage was compounded by the organizers of the event, Neil Hackman[10] and Cynthia Genser,[11] running around the front of the room ostentatiously checking their watches and looking worried. (Something else was scheduled for the stage). My response was to channel energy into Moral Support for Bruce, and to get *very* indignant. After the reading told Cynthia (who was wearing red headband and looking tough and sullen, a la Patti Smith[12]) that I had never on East or West Coasts, been to a reading where the reader was treated more impolitely. She told me "You're fucked!" and then (I found out later) told Bruce she wanted to hit me in the mouth and that he should set me straight. Michael also pitched in his criticisms of the promoters' handling of the reading, so I guess she felt totally threatened. She & Neil were both a part of the group

---

7   A. Aladar Marberger (1947-1988) Art Dealer, director of the Fischbach Gallery.

8   Barbara Baracks (1951-) Writer, editor of the journal *Big Deal*.

9   *High There*. TD's first chapbook, published by SOUP (Some of Us Press) in 1973.

10   Neil Hackman. Poet.

11   Cynthia Genser (1950-) Poet.

12   Patti Smith (1946-) Singer-songwriter and poet.

that went out for drinks at Phebe's afterwards, and although I was pleasant (I was angry at her handling of the reading, not at her—hell, I didn't even know her name until halfway through the evening), she remained miffed. Too fucking bad. Ted Greenwald[13] also was totally disgusted by the performance, although he's scheduled to read there (w/ Jane DeLynn) later in the month.

Saw *Washington Review of the Arts* today, in which Terry Winch lionizes me, in which Steve has (finally!) a poem I really like, in which the DC poetry gang I've just left arrives, as it were, as the poetry establishment of Washington, or at least of the *Review*. Tomorrow going home to close out bank account, do reading Sat. for DC Bicentennial, do reading Sun. at Pila. Book Fair (and on *radio*, I found out today). Last night went to Stud again; 2 really beautiful boys. Tonight went to dinner, Jeff's apartment, East 79th St; terrific meal. Jeff is turning into a very good friend, and I'm happy about that; happy too to be making new friends among other than writers. I'm really trying to avoid dem poem ghetto blues.

---

13 Ted Greenwald (1942-2016) Poet.

15 June:

Last weekend in DC, OK w/ family, *rotten* reading for DC Bicentennial Committee's City Celebration—25 poets under hot sun, w/ cloddish Steve Stevenson running things. *Everyone* was terrible except for Bernie, Harrison Fisher,[1] and *Beth*. And me. Told DeDe Baldwin JA likes her work; she responded so as to let me know she doesn't give a fuck for his. She's so attractive and so utterly humorless and boring. Reminds me of a nun, without the saving gutsiness. Sat. night took train to Philly, stayed at baths, where I had some very intense sex with two guys younger than me who turned out to be hairdressers from Clementon NJ and Harrisburg PA respectively. Got into chests again, got into fucking (in both roles) again too. Ray Pierini was there, tanned & stoned, his usual summer performance, only lots more serious. I went back to his apartment to stay, & Marty Krausz was there. Marty's grown a beard, is very deeply into a monastic venture called The Spiritual Life Institute, which runs hermitages in Arizona and Nova Scotia. The founder is a Carmelite whom Marty kept calling "Father William"—I hate it when title and first name are combined that way, it seems to create & compromise a friendly approach simultaneously. Went to Eagles II for breakfast w/ Marty, then napped at Ray's for a couple of hours and went to ME's[2] for breakfast (I brought bagels). Just realized I had 2 breakfasts that morning. O'Donnell had a cold; we talked politics (she's backing Jerry Brown,[3] which I could not believe). She's coming here to visit on Friday. Next walked to Eakins Oval for the Book Fair, sat at table w/ Michael

---

1 Harrison Fisher. Poet.

2 Mary Ellen O'Donnell. Friend of TD from La Salle College. She appears in the poems "A Fast Life," "For Years," and "Pastorale."

3 Jerry Brown (1938-) Politician. In 1976, he ran as a candidate for the Democratic presidential nomination.

for awhile, bumped into Peter Bushyeager,[4] Joel Colten,[5] Dan Evans,[6] Louise Simons,[7] Dennis Moritz[8] (worthless writing!) and Phyllis, Steve Berg,[9] and cute Albert Mobilio,[10] whose magazine *Clew* is finally out, and is obviously youthful w/ a long way to go. I read on WXPN Radio (John Zeh[11] was MC) with other queer writers, the only one of whom I even *like* is Tommi Avicolli.[12] Read "The Death of a President," and kept in the 4-letter word. Cruised Jeff Moran, assistant editor of *APR*,[13] who liked my work in ZZZ.[14] Michael had a little thing for the man who was obviously Jeff's lover. Hmmm. Much flirtation all afternoon. Albert Mobilio seems to have a girlfriend named Wendy, I think. I bought work by Lorine Niedecker[15] and Allen Fisher[16] from Truck Press. Rode back on train w/ Michael, Ana, & Miles, all of whom were really tired. Randy'd gone to Montreal & had

---

4   Peter Bushyeager (1947-) Poet, writer, editor.

5   Joel K. Colton (1950-1980) Poet and editor. Colton died in the blast from the eruption of Mount St. Helens in Skamania County, Washington, on May 18, 1980. His poems were included in Dennis Cooper's *Coming Attractions: An Anthology of American Poets in Their Twenties* (Little Caesar Press, 1980), for which TD assisted with the editing.

6   R. Daniel Evans. Poet, fiction writer, editor. In 1973, he co-founded (with Louise Simons) the Philadelphia-based literary magazine *Painted Bride Quarterly*.

7   Louise Simons. Fiction writer.

8   Dennis Moritz. Playwright. His selected plays, *Genet at Mettray*, was published by United Artists Books in 2018.

9   Stephen Berg (1934-2014) Poet and editor. Founder (in 1972) and editor of *The American Poetry Review*.

10 Albert Mobilio. Poet and critic.

11 John Zeh (1947-2006) Gay activist and journalist.

12 Tommi Avicolli Mecca (1953-) Gay activist and writer.

13 *The American Poetry Review*.

14 Six of TD's poems were published in ZZZ in 1974: "Mallarmé," "Too Far," "American Baseball," "Gilligan's Island," "President Truman," and "Note to J.A."

15 *Truck 16: The Lorine Niedecker Issue* (1975).

16 Allen Fisher, *Place* (Truck Press, 1976).

been sick there, I found out when I arrived home. Got lots of reading done on all the train rides—finished Jon Strong's[17] novel *Ourselves* and got well into Friedman's[18] *Hermaphrodeity* (at last!).

Yesterday slept late—couldn't really get it together, even when I did wake up. Plotted way of getting lots of old poems in print, spent afternoon in SoHo, mostly talking to Michael & browsing at Jo Hart's bookstore. Sold seven copies of *Sex*[19] to Jordan at the Phoenix, who was bitchy as hell. In evening, dined with Randy at One Potato (awful fried chicken!) then went with Steve Hamilton to see *The Missouri Breaks*. It's a *terrific* film, and I wasn't bored once; don't understand why the film was so disliked by the critics. After movie, we all went to The Stud (Steve's first time); both he & Randy had sex, but not me, for some reason. Ran into Stan, Ed Cox's ex-lover; also blond boy with bow tie from Fischbach party last week, who it turns out is Morris Golde's[20] lover. Morris Golde, it turns out, was one of O'Hara's lovers. I told Steve that Frank O'Hara must have created the New York art and poetry scene single-handedly, with his popular cock.

Today was job-hunt day; went up to Mad. Ave.[21] area for interview with Greg Freson, very nice consultant w/ no job for me but lots of ideas of who might. Saw Gerard Malanga[22] coming out of Public Library, w/ short hair and black briefcase. Michael Andre called and asked me to attend "Magazine" consortium meeting on the 27th to give direct mail advice; it

17 Jonathan Strong, *Ourselves* (1944).

18 Alan H. Friedman, *Hermaphrodeity* (1972).

19 Michael Lally's *Sex/The Swing Era* was published in 1975 as a limited-edition chapbook by TD's Lucy & Ethel Press.

20 Morris Golde (1920-2001) According to his *New York Times* obituary, Golde was a businessman and "friend of arts and artists." Frank O'Hara was a guest at Golde's house on Fire Island when he was struck by a jeep on July 24, 1966.

21 Madison Avenue.

22 Gerard Malanga (1943-) Poet, photographer, filmmaker.

may turn into money so I will. Cards today to Spinner[23] & Tom Farley[24]; rec'd very upsetting letter from my mother, pressuring me to forget about writing as anything important. Thank God I'm away from their loving, ignorant opinions about the future of my life. I listened to *A Chorus Line* straight through, crying at half the songs; then I felt much better.

23 Spinner. Nickname of TD's boyfriend Joey (last name unknown) from Philadelphia. Subject of TD's "Spinner," as well as other poems.

24 Tom Farley. Friend of TD's from Philadelphia. Farley took the photograph of TD that appears on the cover of *High There*.

20 June 76:

It's 3 a.m. or so, Randy sleeping. Just saw some Brakhage[1] films (15, to be exact) and heard Brakhage himself discuss them. I was moved and impressed by the man himself, as much if not more than by the films. His insistence on uniqueness of vision and radical human separation put me in mind of lots of things: of Proust, of Tina Darragh[2] and her talk about The Eyes, of the Spiritual Life Institute in Nova Scotia. Also made me want to go right home & read something serious. Went right home (after stop at 4 and 20 Pies) and had sex, 2nd time today w/ Randy.

So what's happened? Saw *Pacific Overtures* this week, felt "privileged" to be there, developed crush on 2 cast members. Saw *Knock Knock* last night, which was so-so. Had visitors—Mary Ellen & her friend Gary Will came up from Phila. Both Randy & I wanted to sleep w/ Gary, but he & Mary Ellen slept together on our sofa-bed (chastely, I hasten to add). Missed Douglas Dunn[3] performance this afternoon. Missed Rob a great deal this week. Missed Michael's reading in Washington Square w/ Michael Heller[4] & Suzanne Zavrian.[5] Will be missing Steve this summer—he'll prob. be at Naropa as Anne Waldman's[6] secretary, starting early in July. Today's Father's Day—I don't want to let

---

1   Stan Brakhage (1933-2003) Experimental filmmaker.

2   Tina Darragh (1950 -) Poet. TD's close friend from Washington, D.C. See his poem "Stanzas for Martina."

3   Douglas Dunn (1942 -) Postmodernist dancer and choreographer. In 1976, Dunn performed his *Lazy Madge* at Lucinda Childs Studio at 541 Broadway.

4   Michael Heller (1937 -) Poet, essayist, critic.

5   Suzanne Ostro (formerly Zavrian) Creative nonfiction writer, fiction writer, poet.

6   Anne Waldman (1945 -) Poet. Waldman co-founded (with Allen Ginsberg) the Jack Kerouac School of Disembodied Poetics at Naropa Institute in Boulder, Colorado.

that slip by. My story "Waffles" is unfinished[7]—haven't worked on it for a week, & feel guilty over that. Brakhage's comments tonight about the artist letting things besides his work push his work aside made me feel guilty. He also said that artists have rotten social lives, which is not necessarily so—I know lots of artists who lead terrific social lives. Looking over old poems this week to decide what would get sent where, I wondered over "value" of much of it, and of publication in general—but still plan to send the stuff out.

I got out of bed to write all this down—strange feeling of unfulfillment, actual physical hunger, too, although nothing in the house seems to satisfy. Decided this week that not enough of my friends are my own age; what that means on another level, I think, is that I miss and need the comradeship and intellectual stimulation (not even necessarily sexual—in fact, better without it) that people like Jack O'Hara[8] and Frank Tobin provided at other periods of my life. (Called Jack on Friday; he's gotten a scholarship to DC Theological Consortium, and his back is nearly healed). That's not a totally accurate solution; people older than me (Alfred,[9] Michael) have always provided the real intellectual stimulation. What I may be feeling—what I *am* feeling, dammit—is *lonely*. This despite a lover, many caring and interesting friends, and a lot of mental and physical stimulation within easy reach. Brakhage would say Be there, that's where the human being has to be, and what the artist celebrates and fights against simultaneously. But (as I've done since I was a toddler, if my mother's account is accurate), I go on inventing imaginary friends, and falling in love with them too.

---

7 TD eventually finished the story; a typescript is among his papers at Fales Library at New York University. He most likely submitted it to magazines, but the story remained unpublished.

8 Jack O'Hara, TD's friend from Washington, D.C., appears in the poems "The Death of a President" and "King of the Wood."

9 Alfred Ruggerio. Friend of TD from La Salle College. He appears throughout "A Fast Life" and in other poems as well.

25 June –

I'm writing things down here less and less, and will prob. forget or miss a lot—but that may be okay too—the open palm, as opposed to the clenched fist, like waterskiing. So here's what's going on—it's Friday, Tom Wiley & his friends from DC will be staying here this weekend. I'm employed—after much shit from agencies, (incl. a job offer as "editorial assistant" that turned out to be in pornography) I got a call Monday from Galen Williams'[1] office asking me to come in & interview. Cheri Fein[2] is office manager; she told me Brad (heart throb!) Gooch mentioned knowing me & thinking I'm "nice." Was offered job doing mailing list work plus some shitwork for them, which I accepted for 4 days a week. Then went to meet Irena von Zahn[3] at her loft on Wooster St. (she lives with painter named Peter Grass,[4] and is very attractive, red hair! big eyes!). She's doing circulation for Printed Matters, a new publishing firm whose promoters include Sol LeWitt,[5] Carl Andre,[6] & Lucy Lippard,[7] all of whom are supposed to be hot shit (I agree about L.L., don't know the others' work enough to comment). I was still wearing seersucker jacket & tie from morning interview, & I think I came on like Young Forbes Magazine; nevertheless they needed the help, totally—had no idea of what causes what. I'm going to be advising them on a continuing basis. On one night this week (Tuesday, I guess) had dinner with Michael Andre. He called me up & said "Erika is out of town . . ." Went to his loft

---

1 Galen Williams was Executive Director of Poets & Writers, a non-profit literary organization, which she founded in 1970.

2 Cheri Fein. Fiction writer, poet, arts administrator.

3 Irena von Zahn. Artist. Co-founder (with Carl Andre, Sol LeWitt, and Lucy Lippard, among others) of Printed Matter, Inc., a non-profit bookstore, artist organization, and arts space located in Tribeca.

4 Peter Grosz (later known as Peter Grass) Artist.

5 Sol LeWitt (1928-2007) Artist.

6 Carl Andre (1935-) Artist.

7 Lucy Lippard (1937-) Writer, art critic, activist, curator.

first; we sat on couch & talked direct mail, this in preparation for big pow-wow Sunday among 32 little mag editors, at which I'm to be direct mail specialist. M was leaning back on couch a little high, and I couldn't tell whether I was supposed to make a pass or not. Although I really wanted to sleep w/ him when I first met him, now I want him to be a good friend—although I'd still like to sleep w/ him & Erika both (will you listen to this child!) at the same time. We did not touch, anyway; went to Spring St. for supposed opening of Cage[8] show (which didn't happen), then to 162 Spring St[9] for dinner.

I'm not too keen on being back in an office situation, and the work seems like so much flyshit, initially; but I guess I must start from scratch in building my direct-mail empire. Galen is a little spacey, Cheri a little bossy (but nice), others okay, but it's *such* a small operation.

Saw Mike Sappol[10] & Charles Bernstein[11] at St Mark's[12] Monday night; it was a strange combo. Michael was outrageous—I told him he was a breath of fresh air. Charles writes tightly-knit things which sometimes work beautifully: when they allow for full use of breath (not to be Olsonesque).[13] Afterwards went to Orchidea Bar, & to 9th Circle w/ Steve afterwards.

Wednesday made first score in back room of porno bookshop at Christopher and Hudson—strange blond boy from NJ named Gary Lauer.[14] We went out for a walk & to Julius's for drinks

---

8   John Cage (1912-1992) Composer and artist.

9   Spring Street restaurant was located at 162 Spring Street, at the corner of West Broadway in SoHo.

10 Mike Sappol. Writer and editor of *Personal Injury* magazine.

11 Charles Bernstein (1950-) Poet, essayist, theorist, scholar.

12 The Poetry Project at St. Mark's Church in-the-Bowery in the East Village.

13 Reference to poet Charles Olson (1910-1970), who espoused the importance of "breath" in the composition of poetry.

14 In "New York's Numbers," TD writes, "Gary Lauer / from New Jersey with his slouch / and his job selling bargain / menswear in the arcade of the Empire / State Building."

after sex in tiny booth, movie of motorcycle people fist-fucking on screen above our heads. A month ago I'd have thought that was strange, would have felt uncomfortable about it. I still do, but in a different way.

Last night Ted G. and Jane DeLynn read at Sobossek's—dynamite (C. Genser nowhere to be seen). Afterwards, small party at Jane's loft on the Bowery. Bill Zavatsky brought his workshop people—he looks like Carl Reiner, & behaves like him too. I like him, despite the bad things I've heard.

Today was free day—visited Steve at the Strand to pick up copy of *Me & Ralph* by David Sanford, in which he slanders Charlene.[15] Burt Britton[16] showed me his collection of famous authors' self-portraits, and then asked me to do one for him. I was delighted & flattered. Lunch w/ Steve, Michael & Caitlin[17] (who chanced by), then called Charlene about the book. She'll prob. sue, which means I'll have to testify. I'll prob., or poss., write a review of the book.[18] Now to the Park for *Henry V* starring Paul (heart throb) Rudd, & then maybe the tubs. Tomorrow B.

---

15 Charlene Divoky ran Ralph Nader's Public Citizen, a non-profit public interest advocacy group.

16 Burt Britton (1933-2018) Bookseller at the Strand Bookstore in the seventies who would request writers to draw self-portraits for him. In 1976, he published the collection *Self-Portrait: Book People Picture Themselves* (Random House).

17 Caitlin Lally Hotaling (1968-) Daughter of Michael Lally.

18 TD's review of *Me & Ralph: Is Nader Unsafe for America?* appeared in *Washington Review of the Arts* (September 1976). His review includes this paragraph: "In early 1976 Sanford knew that an audit of Public Citizen was in progress. He says he wrote twice and phoned twice to ask for a copy. To one letter, Sanford charges that Director of Public Citizen, Charlene Divoky, responded by saying that 'The auditor had been away.' In broadcast interviews, Sanford has since jazzed up Ms. Divoky's statement, accusing her of having said she 'misplaced the auditor.' To my mind both versions are false. Public Citizen is audited by an outside firm, and there is therefore no staff auditor who could have been away from the office. I was present when the historic phone call was made and, as I recall the incident, Sanford is exercising his imagination about Ms. Divoky's response."

Butterick[19] reads (visited him in bookstore this week; don't know why Ron Schreiber[20] thought him attractive); dinner w/ Albert Mobilio. Also will help M. correct proofs for *None of the Above.*[21] Sunday the Gay Walk. Want to do it all perfectly. Want to eat dinner now.

---

19 Brian Butterick (1956-2019) Performer and poet. Butterick performed in drag as Hattie Hathaway.

20 Ron Schreiber (1934-2004) Poet, editor, educator. Co-founder of the magazine *Hanging Loose*.

21 *None of the Above: New Poets of the USA*, edited by Michael Lally, was published by The Crossing Press in 1976. The anthology includes work by Joe Brainard, TD, Joanne Kyger, Lally, Bernadette Mayer, Alice Notley, Ron Silliman, Patti Smith, and others.

Actually it's 27 June, 2:30 a.m. Happy Gay Pride Day, but since I haven't slept yet I'm dating this Sat. anyway. Albert Mobilio just left; very young and attractive on just about every level. I didn't push the idea of hopping into bed at all; didn't even think to, we were having such a good discussion. I'd like to sleep with him, but tonight was for talk and sharing poems. That sounds ridiculous, but it's true. He's straight, at least to the extent that he has a girlfriend; he also knows I'm gay and isn't at all put off or nervous about that, indicating I don't know what. There's not the tension of the recognition of interest or the straight man's tension in the presence of a non-straight man. Hope this means there's friendship in the works, real friendship.

Last night ended up at tubs after sloppy performance of *Henry V* (Meryl Streep *great*, Michael Moriarty v.g., Paul Rudd & Lenny Baker good, I guess, and the production very sloppy—musicians can't play the long trumpets, body mikes kept failing, actors cracked up in one spot). Had flawless sex—made love, really—with Jonathan Harris, an apprentice with ABT,[1] who was not exactly a stellar conversationalist after an hour of intense genital choreography. Met a Thai student at Parsons named Vit, with whom I talked and who's truly beautiful. This afternoon helped Michael proof *None of the Above*, then went to reading uptown—Shirley Powell,[2] Larry Shorup, Brian Butterick, & Larry Jones.[3] Shirley is a creaky middle-aged dyke w/ middle-western accent who writes pedestrian stuff—Shorup is interesting at points (I told him to read Darrell Gray[4] & Gilfillan).[5] Brian was disappointing—still imitation work. Jones, a big blond with an unpleasant voice, was offensive—read

---

1 American Ballet Theatre.

2 Shirley Powell. Fiction writer and poet.

3 Lawrence Worth Jones (pen name Larry Jones) (1950-) Poet.

4 Darrell Gray (1945-1986) Poet.

5 Merrill Gilfillan (1945-) Poet, fiction writer, essayist. Both Gray and Gilfillan were included in *None of the Above*.

a poem for Anne Sexton[6] that said "you smelled even before you died," or something like that. Now I'm no Sexton fan at all, but that kind of gratuitous punkiness made me *very* annoyed. Told Brian afterwards (for no particular reason) when he asked what I thought of Jones—"Anne Sexton was a friend of mine" and walked away. John Wieners[7] was at the reading—skinny sunburned man with few teeth, who's looking much better than the last time I saw him in Phila. in 72. Shively[8] also there—he looks terrific, w/ moustache and skin cleaned up. Also kind of an Ashberian calm about him—looked a little like JA, even. He showed me the latest *Gay Sunshine*,[9] w/ interview of Kenward and, by Brad Gooch, the review of *Tropicalism*[10] which I was supposed to do but never did. That was the second literary put-down of the day involving Kenward—at Michael's. I found a poem by Darrell Gray I hadn't known existed which uses the same device I do in "Homecoming for Kenward Elmslie"[11] (putting the word "machine" after nouns) to the extent that I'll never be able to publish mine (Gray's has already been printed).

Randy out with guests (incl. Jim Megginson's new lover Clint Hockenberry[12] who works for NSA[13] & who's attractive

---

6 Anne Sexton (1928-1974) Poet.

7 John Wieners (1934-2002) Poet.

8 Charles Shively (1937-2017) Poet and activist. Co-founder of the Boston-based gay newspaper *Fag Rag*, published from 1971 until the early eighties. Michael Bronski: "At the 1977 Boston Gay Pride march, Shively became infamous for burning pages from the Bible—as well as his insurance policy, his Harvard diploma, and a teaching contract—as a protest against oppressive institutions."

9 *Gay Sunshine Journal*. San Francisco-based publication edited by British-American author and editor Winston Leyland.

10 Book of poetry by Kenward Elmslie (Z Press, 1975).

11 Unpublished poem by TD entitled "Homecoming," dedicated to Kenward Elmslie. Gray's poem, "The Poem Machine," was included in *None of the Above*.

12 Clinton C. Hockenberry (1950-1992) AIDS activist, gay rights leader, lawyer.

13 Possibly the National Security Agency.

& *intelligent*, what a relief), doing god knows what. Just struck w/ guilt at not capitalizing God in previous line—I'M SORRY!! Frank Tobin should call tomorrow to let me know about Chris Street March. In previous line, "tomorrow" should read "today."

5 July –

Finding it harder & harder to write here regularly—right now, still mild buzz on from bourbon, my cousin Eleanor & her roommate Maureen Egan, both Sisters of St Joseph from Chicopee Mass,[1] were over here for dinner. I hoisted a few. Trevor came up afterwards to show us his paintings (exciting!)—told us stories of Maxine Groffsky[2] up here clomping around in her Dr Scholl Exercise Sandals. His work is really fine—I told him the adjectives to describe what he's doing haven't been invented yet, and in a sense that's right. Color and composition both very new, although there's a sense of a "tradition" behind the composition.

Last week was Gay Pride Day—I marched in the parade (not meeting Frank Tobin, but meeting Lou & some other familiar faces from DC, including Phil McClain) from Christopher St to 6th Avenue, to Central Park. Then split for meeting of little mag editors at apt. of Sonia Raisiss Giop[3] on upper East Side. Ted Weiss,[4] Ira Sadoff,[5] Joe David Bellamy[6] & other "stars" were there—except they're all so fucking dull they may be anti-stars in some new or very old establishmentarian way. Michael Andre chaired—he's terrific, but seemed so out of place w/ those farts. I acted smart when asked about direct mail, but it's still too early to even talk about doing that. The group decided to call itself Group 34, though some thought the title too flashy—a clue to the tone of the group. Anyway, I'm still their direct-mail person. Went back to village by taxi & had sex in backroom of Studio Bookshop w/ blond kid who gave

---

1 Massachusetts.

2 Maxine Groffsky. Literary agent and editor of *The Paris Review* from 1965 to 1974. Groffsky was the model for the character of Brenda Patimkin in Philip Roth's *Goodbye, Columbus.*

3 Sonia Raisiss Giop (1906-1994) Poet, editor, translator.

4 Theodore Weiss (1916-2003) Poet and literary magazine editor.

5 Ira Sadoff (1945-) Poet, critic, fiction writer, editor.

6 Joe David Bellamy (1941-2014) Fiction writer and poet.

me a little smile & walked away after I'd done him—it's the wholesome ones I have the trouble with. Gay Pride Day made me feel, well, *proud* . . . and such festivities on the street!! Loved each minute. (Marched, by the way, w/ DC people, developed crush on boy from Princeton who was carrying banner w/ a picture of the Washington Monument. *Fag Rag*'s banner read "Fag Rag Cocksuckers."

Monday had dinner at Julius's w/ Alfred Milanese,[7] strikingly handsome friend of Kerry's and poet whose work is influenced by who he reads—at this point, Robert Frost. We went to St Mark's for Steve Hamilton's reading w/ Alice Notley[8]—Steve's later work held together nicely, Alice knocked me out—read w/ much fancy footwork, incl. one piece called "Your Dailiness" which will be in Michael's anthology. Saw Ted Berrigan[9] for first time—much more "middle-aged" than I'd imagined. After reading went to Lady Astor Restaurant,[10] suggested by Charles Bernstein, who'll be away all summer at Ithaca. Then Steve, Alfred & I went to the Ninth Circle, when I set Steve & Alfred up with each other & fell desperately in love (again) w/ Donald Munroe, video artist, who spent 2 nights w/ me in Washington last Christmas. He was in the bar & we talked about having dinner sometime, though neither of us has called yet. Steve & Alfred went off into the night & apparently fucked for 2 days—I didn't hear from Steve until Wednesday. Discovered that Brad Gooch & Cheri Fein (who were at the reading together) sleep together too—imagine my surprise! One more reason to overthrow her (I *hate* my job). Discovered

---

7   Alfred Milanese. Entrepreneur and writer. Milanese: "I had come to New York to be a poet and be part of the poetry scene. I had all of these friends that were doing these wild things. I went on to a job where at least I was only working four days a week. I worked for Revlon for a while as a copywriter. I named lipstick colors. . . ."

8   Alice Notley (1945-) Poet.

9   Ted Berrigan (1934-1983) Poet.

10 Lady Astor's was located at 430 Lafayette Street, across from The Public Theater. Michael Musto: "I loved this charming hangout, which brimmed with chandeliers, mirrors, and hanging velvet."

also that Cheri was tutored one-to-one by Kenneth Koch[11] for a year while in College. Would like to see her work.

Wednesday went to film w/ Jeff & Gary *Murder by Death* on the East Side starring T. Capote,[12] who was sitting 2 aisles in front of us watching himself on the screen! Then ice cream at Serendipity (great!). Night before went w/ Trevor & Gary to Crisco's Disco,[13] where in middle of dance-floor sound bombardment I discovered S&M component of disco music—inexorable beat, sighing, elegant, totally passive & surrendering melody—which *wins*, nevertheless.

Sat. morning went to Michael's to help him finish proofing—Bruce called (he sent me terrific postcard, don't know if he wants to go to bed w/ me or not) & John Duchac[14] called, asking for my number. Sat. afternoon went to 4th of July party at Richard Lautz's[15] in Phila—met people from Key West, R. sat on Lew's lap, ate dinner at restaurant called "The Way We Were"[16] & trained back. Sun. went to see tall ships (200th birthday of America) in Hudson,[17] then to Chris St. Man w/ skin dyed green in statue of liberty drag stopped traffic on West St—no one

---

11 Kenneth Koch (1925-2002) Poet, playwright, professor. Koch taught at Columbia University for over forty years.

12 Truman Capote (1924-1984) Fiction writer and cultural personality. Capote appeared in the 1976 movie *Murder by Death*, Neil Simon's murder mystery spoof.

13 Crisco Disco, a discotheque located at 15th Street and 10th Avenue in the Meatpacking District. It operated during the disco era (seventies and eighties).

14 John Doe (born John Nommensen Duchac) (1953-) Singer, songwriter, actor, poet. Co-founder of the punk band X.

15 Richard Lautz was TD's instructor at La Salle College. His book *Entre Nous* (1982) is dedicated to Lautz.

16 Probably named after the 1973 film *The Way We Were*, starring Barbra Streisand and Robert Redford.

17 Celebration of the United States Bicentennial took place on July 4, 1976 in New York Harbor. Sixteen "tall ships" participated in what was called the Grand Parade of Sailing Ships.

could believe their eyes. Went to Kellers,[18] where Statue ended up, to wait out rain shower, fell "in like" w/ dark-haired boy, my build, red Lacoste shirt, then went to bookstore & had sex w/ long-haired slight boy who was 18 at the most. In evening, went w/ Randy to John Duchac's brother's apt. in Brooklyn Heights to see fireworks designed by Walt Disney—the best I've ever seen.[19] Then took John out, to Mr Wm Shakespeare's[20] (ecch) & 9th Circle, which he liked. John is very closety, but I want to go to bed w/ him anyway, preferably before he leaves for L.A. in September.

Tomorrow, work again. I have the feeling I should be "doing" "more," "getting" "more." But will stay w/ this a short while. Eleanor seemed to have a good time tonight—I'm so much the slave of a family I love but can't deal with on any rational level. I'm running out of paper—it's time to shut this off.

---

18 Keller's Bar, a gay black bar, was located at 384 West Street, alongside the West Side Highway. "There were two pool tables and several pinball machines inside," writes Charles George Taylor. "The floors were wooden, but had slowly rotted over time . . . White men were not permitted inside, unless the bouncers at the door happened to be in a good mood."

19 TD commemorates this moment in "The Fruit Streets," a poem about Brooklyn Heights: "It was here / I smoked a joint with John before he left / to turn into a rock star on the Coast / and watched the fireworks."

20 Mr. William Shakespeare's was a restaurant located at 176 MacDougal Street, off of Washington Square Park. Their "bardburgers" were named after Hamlet, Rosencrantz, and Othello. They also served shepherd's pie and fish and chips.

16 July 76:

After noon, Randy leaves for Cleveland today. My typewriter is fixed, finally; but I'll continue writing this on legal pads. (Alfred in his first letter, c. 1970, told me of his attachment to yellow paper; maybe that's one reason behind all this). Gray day outside; slightly hung over from last night's bourbon and convention speeches. Borrowed Trevor's TV and watched Jimmy Carter's acceptance—I really want to believe him, despite the fact that he misquoted Dylan.[1]

Laundry strewn all over bedroom now; books on every table—all Ned Rorem's[2] Diaries, *Looking at the Dance*,[3] the chapbooks of Terry Winch (from whom a post card this week). My hair wet; dryer not working well either. The left side of my neck from ear to Adams apple is swollen, & throat is sore. Drinks last night (until 9—Randy was upset I hadn't called) with Cheri Fein. Relationship between us is already intense— she has people like George Chambers[4] look at her work, then worries when he doesn't understand it. She worries too over lack of "support system" for work—Brad's about all she has (which I wouldn't sneeze at). This from a woman who was working every day with Kenneth Koch at age 21. It's a lack of confidence I find hard to understand. We were at the Horn of Plenty, by the way.

Could things move into "romantic" sphere now? I think so—fantasized about her last night & this morning. She's very Jewish on the level where self-image takes place, but so am I. And her birthday is the same day as Randy's.

Stood up today for lunch by Chinese lad named Kong, w/ whom flawless sex at tubs on Monday. He's in school at Norman Oklahoma & is going to Europe this Monday on business for

---

1 Dylan Thomas. Carter was a lifelong fan of the poet.

2 Ned Rorem (1923-) Composer and diarist.

3 Collection of Edwin Denby's writings about dance, originally published in 1949.

4 George Chambers. Fiction writer and poet.

his father who lives in Vancouver. Strange places.

Ballet & hamburgs w/ Morris Golde on Wednesday—saw the beautiful Baryshnikov[5] in Twyla's[6] piece "Push Comes to Shove" and with Makarova[7] in "Other Dances." Also Bujones,[8] arrogant & stupendous, in "Bayadere." He's only 21. And Sallie Wilson[9] in "Fall River Legend," which I loved despite its period-piece appeal. Don't think Lynne Dreyer[10] should ever see it, though. Jerry Robbins[11] was on the balcony when we took the air for one intermission—striking looking man. I fell in love w/ most of the corps—the men, to be exact—but no sign of Jonathan Harris, the apprentice I met a couple of weeks ago. Went to Dazzels for hamburgs afterwards. Morris is a Jewish leprechaun, whom I love, with whom I have terrific times. (Brad Gooch says that Frank O'Hara's test of people was whether they loved or loathed Morris—apparently those are the only 2 choices. "Frankie" (as Morris says) was one of M.G.'s lovers at one time, acc. to Steve. It was Steve who introduced us—the 3 of us went to hear Gerrit Henry's[12] songs (partially performed by an awful singer named Robin Charyn) at a Mafia club called Sam's Showplace. Morris knows a lot about the Mafia but is very down on them (a relief). He's leaving for a long vacation next week; I hope to see him before he leaves (said that about Ashbery too every time he's back in town, but never manage to get it together to see him).

Gerrit Lansing,[13] Jane Freilicher,[14] Ned Rorem, John Ashbery,

---

5   Mikhail Baryshnikov (1948-) Dancer, choreographer, actor.

6   Twyla Tharp (1941-) Dancer, choreographer, author.

7   Natalia Makarova (1940-) Prima ballerina and choreographer.

8   Fernando Bujones (1955-2005) Dancer.

9   Sallie Wilson (1932-2008) Ballerina.

10 Lynne Dreyer (1950-) Poet.

11 Jerome Robbins (1918-1998) Choreographer, director, dancer, producer.

12 Gerrit Henry (1950-2003) Poet and art critic.

13 Gerrit Lansing (1928-2018) Poet, editor, critic.

14 Jane Freilicher (1924-2014) Painter.

maybe Steve, maybe me: the alcoholic ("problem drinkers") set, the great New York casualty tradition.

Steve left for Naropa (via Indiana) on Sunday—we have his Warhol cow (autographed to Ted Berrigan) for the summer. Alfred Milanese was up to see him before the flight—can understand A's attraction to S far more than S's attraction to A, even though A is by far the more handsome of the 2.

Rob came visiting on Saturday (his ship was in the harbor), Michael came visiting the week before (Ana was away in Costa Rica & he was really depressed), I went visiting at Ray & Betsi's Sunday night, & subsequently missed Ray's reading at Sobossek's, saw Bruce's reading at St Mark's Monday, wrote letter w/ new poem to Ed Cox, talked to Mary Ellen on the phone, had sex w/ Richard K.[15]

Thoughts for the week—Jim Brodey[16] referring to Tina as "Peter Inman's[17] wife" (they've been married 1 month & already it's started); my reply to Cheri when she told me how straight some male models are—"They've got an image to destroy." Also the bon mots sprinkled by Morris & Cheri throughout their conversations, which I resolved to remember but of course forgot.

---

15 Possibly Richard Kain. TD's "Sonnet" ("a fast life Roscoe's, 4 p.m.") is dedicated to him.

16 Jim Brodey (1942-1993) Poet.

17 Peter Inman (pen name P. Inman) (1947-) Poet. Inman is married to poet Tina Darragh.

18 July –

It's 4 pm on Sunday afternoon, bright day. Brunch with Frank Tobin at Charlie & Kelly's, him wearing red Lacoste shirt & tan military shorts, with little cap. Halfway through our meal, I realize (again) that I love him so much it hurts. He tells me about his off-and-on lover (Ken Shelley[1] of Shelley and Starbuck the Olympic figure skater), about how promiscuous he's been in the last months since he moved into his own apartment; and exudes love for life, for the city, and (I hope) for me. On street he puts his arm around my shoulder, and I wanted to kiss him, but did not. He's moving away from trashing around, which is nice. When he left I felt his absence in my chest and in my throat, just like 2 years ago.

Yesterday sunned on roof in a.m., read Diane di Prima's *Memoirs of a Beatnik* in about 2 hours, then walked to Pier 51, where people sunbathe nude (among other things). Caught the eye of someone tall with reddish hair & freckles [this makes me think of Frank again], and we sat in a window on the second floor watching the cruise ships go by (incl. the Statendam, bearing Rob to Bermuda) for hours. Then came back here (my apt.), had coffee & went to bed—clean salt-water taste of his body. We had dinner together at a great looking restaurant w/ OK food called Chelsea Place, just up Eighth Avenue—ducks swim in their garden, "real ducks!" as every group of diners passing our table near the garden entrance exclaimed. Shirley Stoler,[2] the heavy woman from *7 Beauties* was in the cocktail lounge, and sang along with the piano player. Dan (my new friend's first name—"Hughes" is his last) spent the night here, leaving at 7 a.m. to go to Fire Island w/ friends. I slept then sunned the morning away—perfect weather.

---

1 Kenneth Shelley (1951-) Figure skater. As a pairs skater, he competed with Alicia "JoJo" Starbuck.

2 Shirley Stoler (1929-1999) Actress known for her roles in *The Honeymoon Killers* (1970) and Lina Wertmüller's *Seven Beauties* (1975).

Review of new bio of Celine[3] in *Times Book Review* this morning—I wonder if Peter Inman would be such a fan of Celine's if he knew how anti-Semitic C. was. Also wonder why the anti-Semitism was so important a part of the review, seeing how little of the racist writings are translated into English. One interesting comment the reviewer had, though, was how poorly translated *Journey to the End of the Night & Death on the Installment Plan* are, in their New Directions editions. That comment, plus my renewed interest in Proust & new interest in Roussel[4] & some of Trevor's surrealist and 20s & 30s painting heroes, really make me wish I could read French.

---

3 Louis-Ferdinand Céline (1894-1961) Novelist.
4 Raymond Roussel (1877-1933) Poet and novelist.

22 July –

Nine at night—can't decide whether to go to baths or not. So much time still taken up w/ indecision—yesterday I mapped out a schedule, and of course have broken it already. Right now can't decide where to send my poems. Inspired to send out again, maybe by what's going on at Poets & Writers—mss. coming in, etc.

Monday night went to see Bicentennial Suicide,[1] w/ Simon in the cast, at St. Mark's. It was silly but enthusiastically performed. Ted B & Ted G were there—I went with Danny Hughes, one nice boy. Simon was very into his part, wore blue eyeshadow & lipstick at one point. Called me "my dear" over phone—he really needs *someone* to bring him out, but it won't be me.

Tuesday was down, Wednesday downer—really felt the need to pull my life together, as well as a sense of loneliness. But I realized that I've been leading a very self-centered life in New York, and will have to consciously work at getting over that to actually get over it. Wish there were some "religious" connection I could make at that point. Cheri and Brad have their therapist, an Episcopal nun.

Tomorrow night, dinner at Michael's, with a possible late visit by Keith McDermott[2] of *Equus*. Tuesday night, dinner with John and David. David didn't know who I was when I called up and said it was "Timothy;" "I always think of you as 'Tim,'" he said. Lisa Merrill at the office also comments on my alternate use of the names, as if it were significant. John will be performing with Tom Pasatieri[3] in Vermont at the end of August. I'd like to go up to see that.

---

1 *Bicentennial Suicide: A Novel to be Performed*, written by Bob Holman and Bob Rosenthal, was published by Frontward Books in 1976.

2 Keith McDermott (1953-) Actor, director, writer. From 1974 to 1977, McDermott appeared on Broadway in *Equus*, first opposite Richard Burton, and later Anthony Perkins.

3 Tom Pasatieri (1945-) Opera composer.

I've been reading Cassirer,[4] clear light from Northern Europe, and amazing eyes. Makes me understand *Manfred*[5] and "Heidi."[6] Next (if I can find her) will be Susanne Langer,[7] and Ernest Becker's *Structure of Evil*.[8]

Still have not decided whether to go to the baths!

4   Ernst Cassirer (1874-1945) German philosopher.

5   Lord Byron's *Manfred: A Dramatic Poem* (1817), which takes place in the Bernese Alps (western Switzerland).

6   Children's novel *Heidi* (1881), which takes place in the Swiss Alps.

7   Susanne Langer (1895-1985) Philosopher, writer, educator.

8   Becker (1924-1974) was a cultural anthropologist and writer. The full title of his 1968 book is *The Structure of Evil: An Essay on the Unification of the Science of Man*.

27 July 76 –

On coast of California, in the Dry Tortugas, & other places this past week, whales and dolphins have been beaching themselves at an enormous rate, obviously committing suicide. There isn't any explanation, the scientists say, although despair over pollution of the sea is one theory. It might be what the Baptists call the Rapture, in which we all find out we had a wholly wrong mindset on who the Chosen Ones actually were.

Reading *Language & Myth*,[1] *The Occult* by Colin Wilson,[2] *Monsieur Proust* by the housekeeper,[3] and Nouwen's *Reaching Out*.[4] All deal with the discovery of the same kind of center to a life, the faculty to exercise will in a way which does not preclude the recognition of the subtleties of experience, the dreaming state, or spontaneous insight. Correspondences to Reich,[5] too. I'm trying to learn from all this, trying to listen at least—seriousness of my effort may be cause of recent paranoia (I saw a vampire at the baths last week) and diffuse anxiety. Yesterday at work, keeled over from "hypoglycemic" episode. Also lots of sex in last few days. All this means I'm getting close. And the 2-year cycle of difficulties for Leos that Sharon Thomson[6] told me about has officially begun.

Ten years ago today,[7] Frank O'Hara lay in hospital on Long Island, his body destroyed. Yesterday Reagan picked Schweiker[8]

---

1   Ernst Cassirer, *Language and Myth* (1925), translated by Susanne Langer in 1946.

2   The full title is *The Occult: A History* (1971).

3   Céleste Albaret, *Monsieur Proust* (1973).

4   Henri Nouwen, *Reaching Out: The Three Movements of the Spiritual Life* (1975).

5   Wilhelm Reich (1897-1957) Austrian psychologist.

6   Sharon Thomson. Poet.

7   TD is incorrect about the date, as Frank O'Hara died on July 25, 1966.

8   Senator Richard Schweiker (from Pennsylvania) was Ronald Reagan's vice-presidential pick during his unsuccessful 1976 presidential campaign.

as his running mate—the Mafia team. Last night Ed Cox told me (on phone) about Bill Stafford[9] saying that the art of poetry is to discover the quiet place inside where the poem (already there) can be discovered—corresponding exactly to Graves' "Muse-poetry"[10] I'd been reading about when the phone rang. Colin Wilson talks about poets as "more healthy" than other people, which I don't understand. Also describes the Dolphin-Callers of the South Pacific, who make contact with the dolphins in their dreams and lure them onto shore to be killed & eaten. It works—maybe someone is rediscovering that.

Met Ed White[11] this week—wonderful man. Dinner tonight with John & David. Go to work now. Last night's dreams 1) Angela Lansbury was landlord here & we had a fight. 2) Go back to E.L.[12] & discover some of my teachers were gay, discover my cousin Hank wants to come out, my father discovers my sexual identity & I go into a closet (literally!) to hide from his wrath. The parent locked into the mind of the child, the child perceiving himself as prisoner. At World Trade Center Sunday, man w/ porkpie hat rushed down escalator past me. He was 40 or more, told me "My mother's gonna kill me, I'm late, but I had to come up here again. I love heights. God, I love heights," looking into my eyes for recognition of what he meant.

9   William Stafford (1914-1993) Poet.

10 See Robert Graves's *The White Goddess: A Historical Grammar of Poetic Myth* (1948).

11 Edmund White (1940-) Novelist, memoirist, essayist.

12 East Longmeadow, Massachusetts, where TD grew up. See his poem "East Longmeadow."

2 August:

Thursday I'll be 26 years old. Parents were here this weekend to celebrate. We endured their difficulties with the stairs & with brisk walks—my father's legs, particularly, are giving out. Realized all over again what I've realized before about my parents, which I won't write down right now.

Heavy dreams—Friday a.m. dreamed about my grandfather, much taller than I remember him. Last night dreamed Gerrit Lansing had some power over me—he kidnapped me in Fort Lauderdale (I was on way to Key West) and kept me prisoner in Gothic castle, in France, so I couldn't remember stuff. At end of dream I go to save Randy (also under his spell) only to discover that G. has created duplicates of both of us—Robots or some other kind of creature. Heavy. The night before that, I was fighting organized crime.

Dinner last night in Polish-American Restaurant (that's its name) next to tubs. We went there (to tubs) immediately when parents left—I was a hit, for once, and had a lot of sex, fine sex. Met 19-year-old student at Marist College who told me he thought I was younger than him; he was actually *shocked* when I told him my real age. That made my week!

Cheri's in Vermont today—nice evening with her Thursday at Chelsea Place. Friday, worked at NGTF[1] for first time & found it stimulating, though the office staff is not too friendly. Kenward says he wants me to promote Z Press this fall, so of course I shall.

Last week Jeff came for dinner (steaks cooked on fire-escape hibachi) and Rob dropped in, horny as ever. The 2 of them ended up in the bedroom, then, when I commented on the bad taste of the performance, they moved it to the front-hall foyer. I was expecting Trev to come home & find them entangled.

Phone booth has been put up outside front door; I haven't sunbathed in a week. Reading *Bloodbrothers* by Richard Price; dynamite story that makes me want to get back to "Waffles."

---

1 National Gay Task Force.

Dinner at Ed White's tonight. Trev for din tomorrow. Thursday, Ed Cox visits. In September I am flying to Lexington Ky to do a reading with Anne Maxwell.[2] And that's the way it is, or will be.

---

2   Poet friend of TD from Philadelphia. TD's unpublished poem "Dyke Sonnet" is dedicated to her. In a letter dated "12 Nov or so" 1973 (from Arlington, Virginia), TD wrote to Maxwell: "I went out with **JOHN ASHBERY** on Friday night. He gave a reading at the Smithsonian which knocked everybody out . . . I ended up drinking myself under the table in the company of a great american poet until 3 in the a.m. I think I behaved rather, um, flamboyantly, but he didn't seem particularly grossed out. He told me to 'come up to NYC and see him sometime' which, although I've never particularly approved of the starlet-and-director approach to fame and fortune, is an intriguing offer."

3 Aug 76:

Sharon Thomson on the radio about her work: "I have to get rid of the weak parts of a new poem, the parts where my needs intrude on the needs of the poem." I'm more & more impressed by Sharon Thomson.

Trevor came up for dinner tonight. Talk of John & David (John's doing review of *Tropicalism* for *Parnassus*; also, apparently they left dinner w/ Trev early last night to meet "sexual connection" the same way they did with me on Tuesday). Talk of Jasper Johns, who likes Oriental boys, of Princess Margaret, who likes black boys, and of Lord Snowdon and Prince Charles, who merely like boys, no particular specialty. Talk of Bill Zavatsky, who dislikes boys who like boys, and Phillip Lopate,[1] who sleeps with Julie Christie, who Sharon told me likes girls, at least to the extent of having been to bed with Lauren Hutton. Trevor's trying to get into the Fischbach, and John is writing a letter on his behalf.

I'm trying to get somewhere, not sure of the exact spot—interview tomorrow a.m. with UNICEF,[2] re job. Poets & Writers is a group of nice people, but I have a strong sense of the necessity of dealing in a serious way with my future. Considering the mysterious flu in Philadelphia,[3] that may be presumptuous. I know there'll be an office party at P&W for my birthday Thursday; not a good time to say goodbye.

Last night dined at Ed White's—good food, good company, & I didn't get too drunk. Model named Alec Sawyer, a friend of Don Munroe's from RISD[4] was there; also Michael & Ana,

---

1 Phillip Lopate (1943-) Essayist, fiction writer, poet.

2 From August 1976 to December 1977, TD would write educational and fundraising materials for the U.S. Committee for UNICEF (United Nations Children's Fund).

3 August 1976, the swine flu was considered a possible cause of the outbreak of a mysterious disease in Philadelphia, later attributed to Legionnaires' disease. There were twenty-nine deaths.

4 Rhode Island School of Design.

photographer named Barbara, and (for dessert) Bette Midler's former confidante Patrick Merrill. Keith McDermott breezed in, between *Equus* and (I think he said) the bushes; handsome in a sensitive yet cautious way. His manner reminded me of Kerry MacBride, but when I said that both Michael & Randy were appalled.

More like Tom Breighner, fellow novice years ago, I decided later—which meant I instantly was wary of him.

This morning helped Michael edit a blurb for Franklin Library.[5] This afternoon had lunch with Michael Andre in Central Park (sandwiches). Michael A went skinny dipping with John Lennon this weekend at strange party in Stony Point. We talked about the notion of "models" in painting & literature, and in toys (e.g. a "model" sailboat—what *does* that signify?). I thought of Alec Sawyer—what does *that* signify? M. is going to send me *The Story of the 21st Olympiad*, his latest piece of writing.

Dead so far this week: Fritz Lang, Bultmann[6] (that was last week), ex-president of Exxon.[7] In the Bronx, robbers tied up an elderly husband & wife and put them in a closet. When they were discovered after 5 days, the husband was dead, had been for days. The wife was in a state of total shock. Culmination of 2 human lives.

Mother Teresa is in Philadelphia tonight. I remember her eyes and her bad teeth. One of my fantasies is to join her in her work. Another is to join the order of monks I know exists in NY, who live life of contemplation while living in apartments & holding down secular jobs. I could have written the previous sentence 7 years ago. The 60s have never been resolved.

---

5 Franklin Library was a division of Franklin Mint. From 1973 to 2000, they published leather-bound editions of public domain classics.

6 German Lutheran theologian Rudolf Bultmann died on July 30, 1976.

7 Former Exxon CEO Monroe Jackson Rathbone II died on August 2, 1976.

4 Aug 76, 7:30 a.m.

My dreams: 1) I'm involved in art-fraud scheme in which I smuggle a famous painting out of a museum, then return it secretly. Cheri is one of the people I have to deceive by pretending to be 2 people. She discovers the plot and tells me she's in love with me. We go to bed; Brad Gooch, small, slinky and desirable, watches from another bed in the room as Cheri and I move on each other. He's smiling. 2) My mother calls with "very sad news": Joe Brainard has been killed in a car wreck in Vermont.

6 Aug 76:

It's 1 am, I've passed another birthday, "26" now, making me feel "25" was never where I really was. Job interview this pm with UNICEF—making me wish I worked there, and I might. 2 articles due for *Coda*[1] tomorrow—will they get done? Do I know?

Reading Ed Cox's collected Neruda just now, stumbled on expression "the system of silence," which is a terrific title. Ed's spending 2nd night at apt. of Will Roscoe,[2] student intern at NGTF from Montana. It's good to see Ed again. At dinner last night, Michael told me, he (M) referred to Ed as "butch," which Bruce Andrews objected to vociferously, even though Ed the Fag is butcher than Bruce the Ambivalent in any situation I can think of. They were all discussing me (John Ashbery, Ed White, Bruce & Michael) which I think is nice, especially since (Michael tells me) they said nice things.

Trev gave me a copy of Arthur Cohen's novel[3] and a Duchamp postcard this a.m.; he's off to see Kenward in Vt. for the weekend. I think we (Randy, me, Ed Cox, Will, and Dan Hughes) are going to Fire Island. Just dropped Ed off at Uncle Paul's to meet Will, then went to Stud, got into backroom action with kid who invited me back to his apt. He's a writer, I found out, of fantasy, with Ballantine considering a book. Tentative, basically boring sex—his name's Ed Southwick. Why? Why not— did I do it, I mean. This morning prayed the Office fervently; this evening, a quickie with a man I didn't even find especially attractive. "We" play this out (distancing myself from the events in my life). Told Ed at dinner (Mary's) that time is the tyrant, and that reincarnation talk and drugs are the intellectual and physical way of avoiding that fact. Jesus and Proust were the only people I know to actually break out of the circle; and the

---

1 *Coda* was the Poets & Writers newsletter.
2 Will Roscoe (1955-) Activist and author.
3 Possibly *A Hero in His Time*, published in 1976.

struggles they went through seem too overwhelming for me to even comprehend. So it is by grappling with time, by living in it once, and fully, that "we" are left to deal with it (I said). But I still have those articles to write!

21 Aug 1976:

Fifteen days are not *that* long a time, but it seems like a long time indeed since I wrote in "these pages." Compulsion to keep diary disappeared at about the time I realized I no longer think of myself as "poet." Main event (historical) has been acceptance of new job w/ US Committee for UNICEF, which I begin September 13. I'm excited and a little apprehensive about the job, but vastly relieved to be away from Poets & Writers, esp. my smothering office-mate Bobbie Lazar, who shares my birthday. She's yet another person who uses the "honest and sincere" act to mess around with other people's lives & behavior—very manipulative. Will still be doing Task Force work until October on Friday afternoons.

I want to deal right now with a recent preoccupation with death which has been dogging my waking and dream life. I don't know whether it was because my parents seemed so frail when they visited, but I've been thinking (and have been appalled at the prospect) of my own death and the death of those I love. Dreams last week in which Randy, or Randy and I, perish in plane crash—another in which I refuse to get on a plane I know will crash, & try to dissuade Randy from doing it too. Often I've been waking up in the middle of the night acutely aware of the fact that I will die, afraid it will be soon. Think of Chrissie,[1] of Frank McCarthy.[2] Think also of "preparation" for death, and how to—acc. to traditional formulation? Some of these things I *must* pull together, and (I think) soon.

Last night terrifying interlude. Randy & I were in bed—or *on* the bed, in our jeans—hugging & cuddling, playing around, which led to tickling, which led to wrestling, which led to my covering his face with a pillow. At one point he went limp. I thought he was fooling, but he stayed still. I uncovered his face,

---

1 TD's cousin Christine Spring. Her death is described in "Death Series." See also "For My Cousin, Christine Spring (1948-1971)."

2 Frank McCarthy's suicide is described in "A Fast Life" and "Death Series."

and thought he was unconscious. I screamed and panicked—at which he opened his eyes, he'd been pretending—but I couldn't get control of myself, was hyperventilating, trembling, crying, couldn't speak. This lasted for nearly ½ hour. I was in touch with the extent to which will determines whether "we" live or die—also in touch with the possibility of having destroyed the person I love most, and with the evil something in me capable of that kind of act. My beast. It was an overwhelming experience. To calm me down, we went out to dinner at the Captain's Table later on—but I haven't really calmed down, even yet.

As things stand now, we're going to Nova Scotia for Labor Day weekend—then Randy will fly back & I'll stay on for another week. Worried about the flight, as usual—but not enough not to go. Want to find a little fishing village in which I can breathe, pray, & maybe write a little.

News: talked to Spinner, who's working 2 jobs, one as DJ—he sounded so very much the same. Talked to Bill Appert, Pat Grimaldi, Bob Statler. Lunch w/ Bernie Welt one day, then dinner w/ Michael, Ana, Terry Winch, Bernie, Ted Greenwald, Joan Simon,[3] & Nick De Martino at a restaurant in Chinatown. Letter from Steve in Naropa, who's been living all summer with Alfred Milanese—I feel so *responsible*. Tomorrow, go to Breezy Point to rendezvous w/ Jack O'Hara. Today, had lunch w/ Rob, who's lonely, and sunbathed on the Pier w/ Danny Hughes. Saw *The Blue Angel* for first time tonight, too. Now I go to bed.

---

3 Wife of Ted Greenwald.

29 Aug:

This Afternoon, another run-in with beautiful humorless woman who runs a reading series—this time in the person of one Diane Stevenson,[1] "ex-friend" of Cheri (she said) who handles readings at West End Bar near Columbia. We got into quarrel over P&W's handling of NYSCA[2] money—with her defending the bureaucrats. Kirby Malone[3] was in town to read, his magazine & work both better than I'd expected. He also is very into a "scene" I think; pushing Gerrit's work at the reading, a lovely thing to do. K. read w/ Paul Evans,[4] very fine English poet w/ red hair & beard who's leaving North America tomorrow because of an abortive love affair. Jim Beall[5] came up from DC with Kirby; we're all rendezvousing tonight at SoHo bar owned by Bill Prescott of *Sixpack* magazine.[6]

Last night was restless; hit street & ended up at Stud, where I met a really lovely boy named Jeff, 20 or so, student in English at Michigan State. He came back here & we made love for 3 hours; then he had to go back to parents house in Flushing. He likes Joe's work, so I showed him the paintings on the 2nd floor.

Nova Scotia coming up—was thinking of going back after long weekend, but have decided to spend the long week there, by myself. I'm looking forward to it. Looking forward too to fall—new job, new energy for writing, new shows on Broadway (incl. *Texas Trilogy*,[7] which I never got around to seeing in DC.)

---

1   Diane Stevenson. Poet and scholar.

2   New York State Council on the Arts.

3   Kirby Malone (circa 1955-) Initially a poet, Baltimore-based Malone later became involved in the theater.

4   Paul Evans (1945-1991) Poet.

5   James H. Beall. Astrophysicist, poet, writer.

6   William Prescott. Co-editor (with Pierre Joris) of the seventies magazine *Sixpack*.

7   *A Texas Trilogy* by Preston Jones. It opened in New York on September 23, 1976 at the Broadhurst Theatre, and ran for only twenty performances.

Michael Lally starts work on the same day I do, him as an editor with Franklin Library—what happens to the hippie faggot poets of 73. What else . . . well, Jack O'Hara & Cathy McBride spent the night here this week . . . talked to Tina . . . didn't talk to Don Munroe or Frank . . . and waited for September. We're going to the Pier now; it's sunset.

2 Sept:

Strange, full week. Called Anne & Phyllis Monday—they told me a friend of theirs from Ky, a poet named Jean Feraca,[1] was in NYC trying to get in touch with me. I decided to have a dinner for her—called Ed White, Cheri, Frank Tobin. Then cancelled when 1) I decided it was too close to our departure and 2) I couldn't get in touch w/ the guest of honor. Finally talked to her on the phone tonight—real nice.

Michael, Ana & Trevor for dinner Monday—M & A like T and vice versa. Trev will stay on in NY because of the drought in England. Kenward returns next week.

Went to confession Tuesday—first time in 6 years. Felt good. Felt like expanding spiritual life—we'll see if the resolve lasts. This vacation will be a good testing time. No trashing since then, although I went to Stud tonight after evening where I kept coming on to Will Roscoe at his apt. & he kept coming on to me. Sidelong glances over bourbon, coffee, dope, & Mary Hartman.[2] Nothing happened though. He goes back to Montana next week. Anyway, re Stud—Richard Howard[3] was there, again—the place hosted 2 distinguished writers in one evening.

Found out from Cheri on Mon. that she was the lover of Diane Stevenson, w/ whom I argued on Sunday, and that Diane left her after taking up w/ Phillip Lopate, who also had an affair with Julie Christie, who (Sharon says) had a summer fling w/ Lauren Hutton. The ways of the world.

Saw Keith (finally!) in Equus last night; went w/ Rob. Keith's performance was stunning, better in fact than Tony Perkins. The rather smug & preoccupied dinner companion is one hell of an actor.

---

1 Jean Feraca. Poet, journalist, radio host.
2 *Mary Hartman, Mary Hartman*. The mid-seventies satirical nighttime soap opera starring Louise Lasser.
3 Richard Howard (1929-) Poet, essayist, translator.

Tomorrow we train to Boston. Day after that, we fly to Halifax. I'm so nervous about the flight. But then, it will be fine, I hope; already have reservations for cabin in tiny fishing village of Marie-Joseph (pop. 122) for Monday night. I hope to end up at monastery of Our Lady of Grace—the grace that's gotten me this far, the grace of the morning after sleeping with Rob for the first time,[4] the grace after confession on Tuesday: fifth avenue, sun in the gorge.[5] Back "in touch": then back to NYC for The Season. Told Barbara Baracks tonight that I had to get a new wardrobe for all those openings, & she told me she had to get a new conversation.

---

4 See TD's poem "Second Anniversary."
5 TD's poem "Last Poem, First Morning" ends with "sunfall into the gorge, Fifth Avenue."

DIARY UPDATE . . . 18 October 1976

On way back from the mountains, I run into Ed White in leather jack‹
who's back from seeing Keith in DC, lunch at Lost and Found with
Sir John Gielgud, who then proceeds to porno flick Young Stallior
Richard Horn[1] shows small part of great chest at our first
time together eating hamburgs drinking german beer in small
place on 12th street I don't hear from Morris anymore the dance
goes away Ana goes away today from Michael perhaps I go away
to DC, lunch at Lost and Found in head, lunch in real life
with Spinner at Mr Henry's Georgetown don't want to go back
there any more don't want to go back to the tubs, a dirty place
on 15th street[2] I don't want to go there any more but do
John and Kenward in my living room, David Kermani getting cruise
from Randy in another chair I sleep in apt. near Westbeth where he
lives with Joe Roberts showing small parts of great chest at first
meeting in back room the movie that I love is where they buy a real
boy and go to bed giving pleasure, Richard's favorite is where they
live together in great house, sharing feelings of love and admiration
the way the boys around Ted Berrigan feel in Greek restaurant, a dirty
place on 43rd street Ted says when he met me he thought I was a rur
of the mill queer, but now he's sure I'm way above average, like the Yanks
(what we used to call the Protestants)

---

1 Possibly writer and design critic Richard Horn, who died in 1989 at age thirty‹
   four. Author of *Fifties Style: Then and Now* and *Memphis: Objects, Furniture, and
   Patterns*, both published in 1985. Horn also wrote plays (see TD's November 1
   entry).

2 Probably Man's Country, a bathhouse located on West 15th Street between 5th
   and 6th Avenues. Per Rob Frydlewicz: "Like the other bathhouses, it was mul‹
   level with long, narrow floors. What made it unique, however, was that upon
   entering one of the floors you came face-to-face with the front of a red semi
   with a trailer attached that guys went into to have sex. This floor also held jail
   cells for more role-playing scenarios. A famous billboard for Man's Country
   was in Sheridan Square with the word 'Come!' dominating."

9 Nov 76

Starting a diary is *nothing* in difficulty compared to continuing one after a long absence. It's only been 2½ months, but I find it next to impossible to put pen to paper again for *this* task. Lots has happened. Jimmy Carter was elected President. Patrick Dennis[1] (one of my favorite pop novelists, whom I always thought was *ça va* but who left wife and children) died. I have had, and am still having in some cases, relationships with men named Joe Roberts, Michael Toomey, Richard Horn, and "Joey," a black man in Springfield who has a Scottish last name I can never remember—McLaurin, perhaps. And I am still with Randy, still paradoxically in love with him—he's off in Philadelphia tonight, and will sleep God knows where. We had big election night party, to which came Ned Rorem (whose face looked less parchment-like than when I'd seen him at the P.E.N. O'Hara panel in October) w/ Morris Golde, John Ashbery (totalled—I had to help him downstairs later on) with Tom Weatherly,[2]

---

1   Edward Everett Tanner III (pseudonym Patrick Dennis) (1921-1976) Author of *Auntie Mame* (1955).

2   Thomas Weatherly Jr. (1942-2014) Poet associated with St. Mark's Poetry Project. An unpublished TD poem, "After Tom (Weatherly)," dated "1-9-76," reads:

> when Im a old
> man   poet
> Ill pick up
> th robert pen
>
> warrin wif my
> animals no more
> no more toothmarks
> inside my heart
>
> Ill pose, be wise, write
> about nature, trees
> but til then I aint
> got th time

Jane DeLynn, Cheri, Brad, Richard H, Randy de Leeuw, and his young man Bill Gilroy, Ed White, Joe B, Maxine Groffsky, David Kalstone,[3] Michael (who has been jilted tragically, by Ana, who's staying at Larry Kert's[4] apt. a couple of blocks from here), Gardner McFall,[5] Betsy Sherer (about whom more later), Bruce & Ellen,[6] Ray & Betsi, a painter named Denise Green,[7] Don Munroe & friend, Steve and Alfred (still together!) Frank,

---

3 David Kalstone (1933-1986) Writer and critic. Kalstone died of AIDS at the age of fifty-three. TD wrote the following poem on November 27, 1988:

> **West 22nd Street**
>
> Lapsang souchong
>
> the favorite tea
>
> of David Kalstone
>
> has a *purple* taste
>
> on a winter day
>
> in 1976
>
> in a parlor crammed
>
> with books
>
> one of which
>
> (*Women of the Shadows*)
>
> I'll never return

4 Lawrence Frederick "Larry" Kert (1930-1991) Actor, singer, dancer. Created the role of Tony in the original Broadway version of *West Side Story*.

5 Gardner McFall (1952-) Poet, children's book writer, librettist.

6 Bruce Andrews's wife at the time.

7 Possibly Denise Green (1946-) Artist and writer.

John, and oh who else? Erin.[8] It was a *great* party, and I passed out halfway through it about 2:30.

I've been writing a little review for *WROTA*,[9] column for *Christopher St*,[10] plus occasional poems—and direct mail letters for UNICEF, which I enjoy. Have been more in touch with my feelings for women, esp. Betsy Sherer, with whom I work, & Cheri, with whom I used to work. And always in touch with what remain of my feelings for men. Went to tubs w/ Randy last night—the beautiful selfish people (of whom I'm one) were there. Had sex "almost" to the point of "the Big O" (Betsy's expression) with 4 people, all of whom either came and lost interest immediately or didn't come and lost interest immediately. I came home "unsatisfied" (which I would have been even if I'd gotten off) and angry. Oh well.

Went to Boston to visit Mike Toomey this weekend & realized it is the 3rd time in 4 years I've been there on exactly that weekend. Thought a lot about Patty[11]—tried to call her friend Ken Rivard, w/ no luck, to see if he knew how she was doing. Tried again from here (home) just now—again no luck.

I'm back into Catholicism after another short vacation—despite having spent Sat. w/ Joe O'Hare in Weston[12] & being depressed at his "seminary life" and the way he seems to be coming apart. Mass 2 days this week—I want to keep it up. Brad was confirmed Sunday in the Episcopal Church, so there are 2 in "the gang" into "it." I lent Richard, with whom l'affair seems to be over, my copy of Merton's *Contemplative Prayer*.[13]

Lots more has happened, but I don't like catching up. From now on, on and up—or at least, on.

---

8   Possibly Erin Clermont (1943-) Writer and editor. Clermont is mentioned in TD's poem "On This Train Are People Who Resemble."

9   *Washington Review of the Arts.*

10 The gay magazine *Christopher Street.*

11 Possibly the Patty mentioned in "A Fast Life."

12 Weston Priory in Weston, Vermont. Years later, in July 1988, TD spent a week there and kept a diary, "Weston – Retreat Notes."

13 Thomas Merton, *Contemplative Prayer* (1969). A now classic spiritual text.

13 Nov:

Yesterday found out that Burt Britton included my self-portrait in his book of self-portraits by writers. I was amazed and delighted, of course; went to Strand after work yesterday and picked up a copy which B. signed. The party for it is next Monday—that is, Monday a week.

Michael sent me a vicious review that Hayden Carruth[1] did of *None of the Above* singling out Ray's work for special mention. I'd like to respond at length, and Michael would like me to also, I think; but I really can't, seeing as how I'm in the book. But if Dick Higgins[2] and Carruth dislike the work equally, then it's in exactly the place on the continuum that it should be.

Went to Philadelphia Thursday night with Betsy to check on lettershop in S. Jersey, terrible mess; then drinks at Lickety Split and dinner at Three Threes, first time *there* since w/—Tim?—in 1972 or so. It hasn't much changed. Betsy fills my fantasy life right now; I think I'd really like to start a relationship with her. Don't know *what* would, or will, happen though.

Today I'll work for a few hours at UNICEF (even though it's Saturday—don't like that at all), then hear Sharon Thomson read at Chumley's, then go to Glen Baxter[3] opening on 57th St, then meet Richard here and go to see Mabou Mines[4] do *Cascando*[5] at the Public Theater. Also, Tom Farley and his lover Steve will be our houseguests this p.m. Hi-ho the glamorous life.

Tried to write poem for Richard this a.m.—it self-destructed in midstream. I'm thinking of plot for short story based on Tina's weekend w/ Nigerian cab driver, my old plot for short story "Waffles," and plot outline for my (supposed) collaborative

---

1   Hayden Carruth (1921-2008) Poet, literary critic, anthologist.
2   Dick Higgins (1938-1998) Poet, composer, artist.
3   Glen Baxter (1944-) Artist.
4   Experimental theater company in the East Village.
5   Radio play by Samuel Beckett.

potboiler with Chuck Ortleb[6] (*The President's Son*). Thinking also of Mother Cabrini—Friday's her feast, and the Office of the day is incredible in its antisexuality ("bed of sin" is one phrase used) and the attention it pays to her virginity; rather than her accomplishments. Fucked up, I'd say.

Now it's time to shave, drink tea, and go to work.

---

6   Charles Ortleb (1950-) Writer and publisher of the monthly gay magazine *Christopher Street* (1976-1995) and the biweekly gay newspaper *New York Native* (1980-1997).

16 Nov 76

Difficult to take the time to write these things down—difficult tonight especially. I've been dragging all day hung over from last night—plunging self in work. Dragging too over having another emotional crisis intrude on my life at this point—this one over deciding what to do with my feelings for a woman, who reciprocates those feelings. Last night Betsy and I were drunk at the DMFA[1] auction—went out afterwards with Stephen and Adrian, and Betsy told me she thought she could fall in love w/ me very easily. We ended up kissing and holding hands in her car and over cappuccino at Sandolino's, she crying. I have not felt so tender toward anyone for years, and it hit me so hard it came like a new feeling. Now we've both got to deal with it.

Became contributing editor of *Christopher Street*[2] tonight. Burt's book party made *Vogue*; he (and 699 authors and me) are minor celebs. I'm too exhausted to write more.

---

1 Direct Marketing Fundraisers Association.

2 Beginning in December, TD would write a monthly column for *Christopher Street*, "Rough Trade," featuring "behind-the-scenes news of the publishing world that involves gay books and books of interest to gay people."

19 Nov

5:30 am, I wake up bombed out (still) from last (this) night and bummed out over what happened. After 4 drinks at "Unimail" party met Richard for *Cascando* at the Public Theater, and he almost immediately informed me that he's in process of relationship with Lou Rispoli,[1] whom I was drunk enough to say I can't stand. Lou and I end up in competition constantly, over a number of things—and he's so fucking mediocre on almost every level that it annoys the hell out of me to keep being in that situation. I know that's elitist and uncharitable as hell; it's also true. Well, Richard and I disagreed over the play, then cabbed to Duff's for dinner (Joe B. and Anne Waldman were there) at which I ended up paying most of the tab, as usual in these situations, and we talked about Lou Rispoli which I didn't want to do. (Does this all sound bitchy? It *feels* bitchy.) Then we came back here, the invitation to Richard's apt. disappearing somewhere along the way, and I read Act I of "The Human Sacrifice"[2]—very tight and good—and found out (after dealing w/ trying to find a theater) that R. had reneged on his offer of my acting in the play when it was produced. We made out a wee bit, then he was tired and went home. I pounded bed in

---

1   Gay activist Lou Rispoli was sixty-two years old when he was murdered (in a possible anti-gay hate crime) in Queens, New York, in 2012.

2   Possible play by Richard Horn.

rage for awhile (felt good) and collapsed.[3]

Tonight I have to deal with being at theater knowing Betsy's out with 35-year-old named Bob, and may or may not sleep with him, which although I have no corner on her market also annoys the hell out of me. We had lunch at Uncle Charlie's on Thursday and decided to "pursue it," but because of hectic schedules I won't see her 'til Monday. Keep wanting to call her, but that would be uncool.

After talking to Bill Enters at party tonight (he's doing

---

3   TD's feelings about Richard Horn (and Betsy Sherer) are expressed in this undated and unpublished poem:

> I couldn't live
> anywhere else, the sky
> has been described 100,000 times
> but it still takes me out
>
> down here on the river it's
> cold, hard
> to write it down and take it in
> at the same time
>
> Emilio Cubeiro
> Hart Crane
> Simon Schuchat
> Brad Gooch
>
> Betsy Sherer I'm in love
> with you this morning
> Richard Horn I'm furious
> at you but it will pass
>
> S. S. Oceanic
> big white ship
> passes by reflecting
> morning sun
>
> I'm the only one
> here, here
> it smells like the ocean
> but it's only a very wide river

mailings for a technical correspondence school) I told Jo that there were 3 kinds of mailers—the good, the bad, and the trivial—and she agreed.

Postcard today from Clay Fear,[4] glad he was mentioned in *None of the Above*, says Rae Armantrout[5] likes my work. (Kathy Acker's[6] videotapes were shown at Whitney this week, by the way). And Cheri tells me Ned Rorem didn't much like the anthology—he said "I still haven't picked up all the 'I's that fell out of the book onto the floor" or something like that. Thinking hard, the only "I" poets in there to any extent are Michael, Joe, and to some extent Alice Notley—and they're both doing other things than being self-indulgent. So "I" guess N.R. just means we're young and threatening, the way he used to be.

---

4   Clay Fear (1948-1997) Fiction writer. Author of *I Don't Expect You'll Do the Same* (chapbook with a black-and-white photo of an erect penis spanning the back and front covers, published in 1974) and *Susan Hayward has brain surgery, or, As the music faded*. TD lists him as an influence in *None of the Above*.

5   Rae Armantrout (1947-) Poet.

6   Kathy Acker (1947-1997) Experimental novelist, playwright, essayist.

23 Nov 76:

1st ish[1] of *Christopher St* w/ my work out, looks fine. Just back from Donna Dennis[2] opening, Randy starred—Taylor Mead[3] tried to set him up w/ "Larry," who worked w/ Jackie Curtis's[4] play at La MaMa. Larry wanted a 3-some, but I said No. Anne Waldman danced w/ Alfred at the opening, I talked to Brooke Alderson[5] & George Schneeman,[6] & cruised for a while w/ Jane DeLynn. Was attracted to a blond boyish person whom I thought was a man—it turned out to be the lesbian lover of Jane's ex. Donna Dennis has been to bed w/ Jane DeLynn, used to go out w/ Ted Berrigan, & is attracted to Michael Lally. I think she's very cute. Betsy was supposed to go to opening w/ me, but she has (I fear) the flu.

Big weekend—Kathy Acker's tape and *Porgy*[7] on Sat (both fine), then dinner w/ Stephen Patrick and Adrian Glass at Daley's. Sunday drinks w/ Richard, Brad, Cheri & Rachel, then *Einstein on the Beach*[8] at the Met. Incredible show, both in theater & lobby. Saw Steven Hall,[9] John A, Sandy McClatchy w/ Alfred Corn, James Merrill[10] (death on toast, looks-wise), David Kalstone, Maxine G, Ed White & Keith, Victor Bockris,[11]

---

1 Issue.

2 Donna Dennis (1942-) Sculptor.

3 Taylor Mead (1924-2013) Writer, actor, performer.

4 Jackie Curtis (1947-1985) Actor, writer, singer, Warhol superstar.

5 Brooke Alderson. Actress who appeared in the movie *Urban Cowboy* (1980). Married to art critic and poet Peter Schjeldahl. See TD's poem "No Sympathy."

6 George Schneeman (1934-2009) Artist.

7 A revival of *Porgy and Bess* was playing at the Uris Theatre on Broadway.

8 Two performances of the Philip Glass opera were held at the Metropolitan Opera House in New York in November 1976.

9 Steven Hall (1957-) Poet. His work appears in *Coming Attractions*.

10 James Merrill (1926-1995) Poet.

11 Victor Bockris (1949-) Writer.

Alfred Milanese—who else?? Ed White next day said he was still "trembling," and with good reason—the opera was unbelievably moving and gorgeous. Everyone in the theater knew we'd (the culture) turned a corner.

Last night Steve H and I were on cable TV, about which the less said, the better. Then to NGTF meeting for me at Robert Livingston's[12] penthouse, followed by Burt Britton party at the Strand—met Vonnegut,[13] missed Joel Grey. Dreamed—is that the word?—of Pres. Kennedy at night—it was much clearer than a dream. Terry & Doug[14] were in town for Burt's party. Jamie Auchincloss's[15] father died yesterday.

Tomorrow to DC, so won't be visiting here 'til after Thanksgiving. Am rereading Yeats's *A Vision*, and this time may learn something.

---

12 Robert L. Livingston was a co-founder, in 1973, of the National Gay Task Force.

13 Kurt Vonnegut (1922-2007) Writer.

14 Probably Doug Lang. Poet, writer, publisher. His Jawbone Press published TD's chapbook, *For Years*, in 1977.

15 James Lee Auchincloss (1947-) Half-brother of Jacqueline Kennedy Onassis.

Thank You

Bryan Borland, Jane DeLynn, Brad Gooch, Cora Jacobs, Bethany Kanter, Michael Lally, Seth Pennington, Peter K. Steinberg, Tony Trigilio, Bernard Welt, Terence Winch, Christopher Wiss.

ABOUT THE AUTHOR AND EDITOR

Tim Dlugos was a prominent younger poet who was active in both the Mass Transit poetry scene in Washington, D.C., in the early 1970s and New York's downtown literary scene in the late seventies and eighties. His books include *Je Suis Ein Americano* (Little Caesar Press, 1979), *Entre Nous* (Little Caesar, 1982), and *Strong Place* (Amethyst Press, 1992). He died of AIDS on December 3, 1990, at the age of forty. At the time of his death, he was pursuing graduate studies at Yale Divinity School. *A Fast Life: The Collected Poems of Tim Dlugos*, edited by David Trinidad and published by Nightboat Books in 2011, won a Lambda Literary Award.

David Trinidad's books of poetry include *Swinging on a Star* (Turtle Point Press, 2017), *Notes on a Past Life* (BlazeVOX [books], 2016), *Peyton Place: A Haiku Soap Opera* (Turtle Point, 2013), and *Dear Prudence: New and Selected Poems* (Turtle Point, 2011). *Digging to Wonderland* is forthcoming from Turtle Point in 2021. He is also the editor of *A Fast Life: The Collected Poems of Tim Dlugos* (Nightboat Books, 2011) and *Punk Rock Is Cool for the End of the World: Poems and Notebooks of Ed Smith* (Turtle Point, 2019). Trinidad lives in Chicago, where he is a Professor of Creative Writing/Poetry at Columbia College.

ABOUT THE PRESS

Sibling Rivalry Press is an independent press based in Little Rock, Arkansas. It is a sponsored project of Fractured Atlas, a nonprofit arts service organization. Contributions to support the operations of Sibling Rivalry Press are tax-deductible to the extent permitted by law, and your donations will directly assist in the publication of work that disturbs and enraptures. To contribute to the publication of more books like this one, please visit our website and click *donate*.

www.siblingrivalrypress.com

www.ingramcontent.com/pod-product-compliance
Lightning Source LLC
Chambersburg PA
CBHW022040090426
42741CB00007B/1135